Praise for
Negative Money

"Lillian-Yvonne Bertram once again reveals how they are light-years embedded inside the lyric, a futurity grounded in a currency of creation, resistance, and voicing of multiplicity. In short, they are their own blockchain of language: 'I have visions of honey / in my eyes.' *Negative Money* exhibits a disruptive poetics that hacks hidden chambers of viewing, of how we connect and understand ourselves and others."
—MAJOR JACKSON, author of *The Absurd Man: Poems*

"This book blew me away. It is brilliant, funny, wounded, intimate, strong, vulnerable, electric, and completely original. I want to hand this book to everyone I know and say: This is what poetry can do." —MATTHEW ZAPRUDER, author of *Father's Day* and *Story of a Poem*

"*Negative Money* engages a spectrum of interrogation into the poetic form's intentional discourses to dismantle power. These beautifully crafted poems look at the way power relations are set up in whiteness, academia, and gender, articulating how the body can be consumed, exploited, hurt, and adjudicated; they build an emphatic affective world that both cries out and governs its necessary reckoning."
—PRAGEETA SHARMA, author of *Grief Sequence*

"I've been a big fan of Lillian-Yvonne Bertram's poetry since their first collection, *But a Storm Is Blowing from Paradise*, in 2012. Since then, they have written one stunner after another, experimenting with the page like a word alchemist. Along the way, they reframed how social and political critique work in concert with poetic destabilization. Their brilliant new collection, *Negative Money*, reminds me of a poetic rumble between Terrance Hayes and Harryette Mullen—their unexpected music, their insistent allusions, their grand awareness that things stay silent only when we stay silent. Each poem in the book is more significant and challenging than the previous as they build an open-eyed critique of capitalism, American violence, gender, and race. If you haven't read Lillian-Yvonne Bertram yet, *Negative Money* is your opportunity to fix that and, as Jimi Hendrix said, pick up on it." —ADRIAN MATEJKA, author of *Somebody Else Sold the World*

Praise for *Travesty Generator*

"Bertram brilliantly conveys how Black experience becomes codified, homogenized, and branded for capitalist dissemination. Code, written by white men, is part of the hardwired system of white supremacy, where structural violence begets itself. But Bertram hacks into it. They re-engineer language by synthesizing the lyric and coding script, taking the baton from Harryette Mullen and the Oulipians and dashing off with it to late-twenty-first-century Black futurity. *Travesty Generator* is genius." —CATHY PARK HONG, author of *Engine Empire* and *Dance Dance Revolution*

"*Travesty Generator* powerfully breaks and remakes contemporary poetry's 'small machine of words.' Timely in its sociopolitical critique and visionary in its formal inventiveness, Bertram's collection offers a guide to a poetics of the new Afro-future." —JOHN KEENE, MacArthur Fellow and author of *Counternarratives*

"*Travesty Generator* is so carefully crafted and considered from a standpoint of musicality. Where some would consider the voice as the sole instrument, Lillian-Yvonne Bertram understands language as the true vehicle for instrumentation. These poems sprawl generously, drift a reader seamlessly between percussive urgency and gentle harmonies. The words cascade until entire symphonies are created. What a joy to see a book this brave and unafraid of its own many possibilities."　　—HANIF ABDURRAQIB, author of
They Can't Kill Us Until They Kill Us

"*Travesty Generator* uses computational processes to demonstrate that randomness offers no escape from the patterns that grief and outrage form in Black lives. Composed with (and sometimes of) permutation programming code and algorithms, these poems run relentless procedures on the language of Black death and Black survival. Bertram's poetic 'output' will confuse and frustrate you, then mesmerize and haunt you—feelings generated by the poetry, as by the very terms of Black life in this country."
　　—EVIE SHOCKLEY, author of *Semiautomatic*

NEGATIVE
MONEY

NEGATIVE MONEY

poems

LILLIAN-YVONNE BERTRAM

Soft Skull Press
New York

First Soft Skull edition: 2023

World Maps graphic design provided by Thirada Chanawichote

Library of Congress Cataloging-in-Publication Data
Names: Bertram, Lillian-Yvonne, 1983- author.
Title: Negative money : poems / Lillian-Yvonne Bertram.
Description: New York : Soft Skull Press, 2023.
Identifiers: LCCN 2022056808 | ISBN 9781593767532 (trade
paperback) | ISBN 9781593767549 (ebook)
Classification: LCC PS3602.E7685 N44 2023 |
DDC 811/.6—dc23
LC record available at https://lccn.loc.gov/2022056808

Cover design by www.houseofthought.io
Cover image by Kyohei Matsuda
Book design by tracy danes

Published by Soft Skull Press
New York, NY
www.softskull.com

Printed in the United States of America
10 9 8 7 6 5 4 3 2 1

For my parents

It was not precisely grass but it was green

PAUL KLEE

Contents

NEGATIVE MONEY

Demagogue Money

I cannot bear pigs.
  Sensational pig and his
    black foods stomp to some top.

False sonatas spit raging.
  The chatter of our troubles is an aspect
    of breath, glass pulled from fire,

the wool of our ensemble.
  I cannot bear time.
    In the each other

there is this desperate we
  crying down and across
    each other, getting older.

Getting closer is the room behind
  the door before the door
    to it gets worse.

There are moments
  I cannot bear law and its
    hot white golden rattles.

On the street we hiss.
  On the street we blare.
    In white directions

America is expensive. On the street
  we eat. Its malnourished sermon
    the cabinet of our chains.

the river it shines pure white

the professor jokes that he'll leave me   "somewhere"
       around   Danville   somewhere   along   the
banks of the Wabash   he raises his eyebrows in a
joke   Wabash from *Oubache* from
the original *waapaahsiiki* "you know, around sundown"
      waapaahsiiki meaning *pure white* or *it shines white*
                        or *water over white*
              stones
around those sundown towns "see how you like it" It's just
       Illinois
     we take long drives   to get something   or other:

a bag of feed   a set of stakes for a fence   a rope for a
       dog tie
a set of golf clubs   huevos   rancheros   and   biscuits
       he jokes
       laughs
"it's not personal"   I dry into the seat like a seed   laugh
     yes I can   take a joke   we are
friends   I yoked a long laugh   laugh along   It's
Illinois
      two-thousand-seven   Tuesdays are tornado siren
tests
It's not personal
     the news about this surprising   senator
Black member   of a legislating body   It's not
personal
     "he's so   (for   one   of   *them*)
     articulate"

I am a student   I'm helping out   it's my
job   picking   up   the   visiting   writer
        It's Illinois
two-thousand-something
                the   b&b's   big   business   is   in   visiting
        professors
        harvest season air   all but combusts
                I'm waiting in the lobby   where
the white proprietress   says   I impress her
        I'm so
articulate

                                            It's Illinois
two thousand and
        she prefers   lighter people   It's   not
personal
I'm wearing some   but not too many   gold hoops
the visiting writer appears
        in her long black dreads   at the top of
the stairs

                        It's not personal   but I didn't
                again go to give that place   business

It was Illinois   It was never   personal   Not
        about me   the   professor   refusing   a
recommendation   tho   we   passed   for
friends   drove long stretches in the country
                white stars passed overhead

                        choked   the   night   ash   of
        pasture burn

(5)

I can take   an "it's not personal"   joke
         It's not personal   I mean nothing
mean
         in remembering   *to those who would*
               have the clubhouse but I have not
                         forgotten   even
now
         I am apologizing
for   this colored memory   testing sirens   It's
Illinois
         I told the professor   how I was
mesmerized by the corn
         it's why I came   Midwest   I wanted
to know
what in all   it's been whispering   about   prosperity
         whispering all this time   about freedom
coming in
      waves   like heat off tar   I search the Illinois
skies for funnels   stand three
days a week
         in front of   twenty-two white students   stand
like a strip of
         It's not personal   like a strip of black
electrical tape   pressing wire to a   white wall
I
         listen for the storms   tornados   they say   sound
like imagine   you are facing   a train

The Grains of Ascendancy
an abecedarian

AgriGold squares the county roads in miles
        & not since Solomon is production so
Biblical: roots deepening into kernels, crops reflecting
        rotational laws.
Consider the traits of cops, crosses, and roses:
        how this scenario reflects all-American scientists
        zeroed in on the
Diversity of wheats, grains dry-husked and rubbed to a
        staticky charge. In this weather so
Extremely of the late century, I count every presence, every
        ever-present penis skimming the dialogue, and my
Fussy bungles the tenured denouement, irritating seasonal
        growing patterns. Yet the chemicals and musk
        stagger to their
Greatness. Yell over the world that the indigenous will in-
Herit the earth and some subsidized Custer will till you
        under with a tweet.
I can't breathe for all this modern wheat stoppering my
        nostrils. I await the American agriculturists to
        address the
Issue of this
Intolerance. West of Independence,
Jefferson City holds the World's Only Corn Palace (closed
        for renovation on my visit). To
Kill time I bought a pink "Police Girl" cap gun
        & a five-point tin sheriff badge. Let's play *Freeze!*
        or *I'll*
Light you up.
Mankind came to modernity on the whittled backs of grain.
        Blame guts on gluten,
        revolution on

Night sweats, night sweats on red summer, Red Summer on
     Red May, Red May on the wheat wave, wheat wave
     on easements easing
Open leagues of frontiers, homesteaded hectares proofing
     with bloom. Milling
Punishes grain and calls it "progress." This night is Illinois-
Quiet, save for the mill train and alfalfa fields shushing the
     air. *If I die in police custody,*
Return me to my mother as a blood-soaked sock full
     of batteries. This night is canyon-quiet, is Maine-quiet
     & lobster-
Shell red, the color of battered flesh
Too changed to ever change back. *Unhealthy wheat culture
     means civilization is in decline, and if we're gone,
     this whole playhouse goes*
Up in smoke, and who left will pollinate these
Vacant hulls. *I see green fields . . . but I can't seem to get there
     no how.*
Wheat can but we can't winter here. With allies like these,
     who needs anthra-
x. Can
You survive every gotdamn thing? Centuries in, centuries out,
     the roller mill revives colonial wheats. The germs
     of revolution collapse to flap like cards in the
     spokes of
Zarathustra.

How Narrow My Escapes

I may still have been

a girl then & a cheap drunk
          watching opossums
dance like ghosts under the moon

of another harvest weekend.

When I slept in the cornfields,
          I went two years with no
sex. For this the boys

declared me leaf or

          stem cutting, graft to rootstock.

No one knew

where to look for me
          but who was ever looking.

I staged my portraits:

          hung myself, neck out
of view, a shade

in the making.
          In the long exposures
I clinched at my flimsy

shadows:
       us doubled up in the stupid
shirtdress

that never fit
       my hips,

kitten heels I'd one day

vomit on

in downtown Brooklyn,
       just like a real girl. Please
don't tell

my mother
       what she already knows—I
had to

reinvent the well,
       dedicate each spade's heap
to the starry bottom

& there you'll find me still,

dreaming that rain
    follows the plow.

       Did I year wrong? My student
tells me

we are in the *last days,*

      that God will pour out
his seven bowls

of Armageddon:
      a just punishment
for the wicked. *The end*

of the world is near,
      he points, *look around and*
you will see the prophecy

fulfilled.
      I look around & see
that making it on merit

is a wooden
      nickel and my cup
of wine
      is filled with holy air.

Did you not know

that to anoint someone

      your last love is to
tempt them

to flight?
      Alone I drink and drink
under my cracked

lacquered
      tiles of pride. Whole days I
send this tongue

around my teeth
      but nothing gives up
its hiding place.

Once, I had two dreams:
      one *lazy*, the other, *away*.

—the dream world is a place Lillian can reach through the body

For Lillian, their Black body is both fleshy material, which exists in the material world, & social construct. It has a special place. As Maurice Merleau-Ponty said, "The outline of my body is a frontier which ordinary spatial relations do not cross," although for the Black body it is a frontier always crossed, or at least threatened, by members of the "human family," the gaze of men in a park, or in Lillian's own fantasies. The more present Lillian's Black body, the more Lillian responds to people watching them in a park, & Lillian enters a dream world where they can escape to the outside of the limitations of raced, gendered, & sexualized public space. The range of possibilities offered by the dream world, as against the limitations of the daily, is illustrated by the repeated ampersand. From a particular person in a particular place & with all the restrictions that brings, & where Lillian is located through their previous relationships to the place & the people in it, the Black body & the poem about the Black body become a space of possibility. Like the ocean. Like a continent. It is a place in which "I marry in, then out. / Under it I stroll, a sky so blue and visible and starred" (Lillian-Yvonne Bertram, *a slice from the cake made of air* [Pasadena, CA: Red Hen Press, 2016], 72). It is a place that makes action possible, but not compulsory, a place in which Lillian can do, or not do, what they like. Yet for Lillian, pleasurable though the abstraction might be, & whether it takes Lillian to some place else such as the imagined geography of "over there" or the eroticized fantasy of the dream world, the Black body must still exist between the immanent experience of everyday life & the possibilities of the abstractions of the transcendent as when Lillian says, "You hope it's not true" (Bertram, 72).

(13)

My Past Has Value

to the men who never knew me
then. If pretty now, think how pretty when
so newly wounded in a world.
They paid for rent,
spent hundreds on this girl's birthday steaks.
                    Men away from wives
on work trips are simple men
with simpler desires. Of what did I
remind them? To the first man who checked
me out in the corner bookshop at thirteen
& left ten dollars at the counter
for this girl —thank you
                    for funding Vonnegut,
                    Bukowski, and Freud. Men

on the shelf of men who told me
what to think, men who toyed
with drunk too much, drive too reckless,
who interpreted for me
all my dreams.
To the man who said I was too much
hyperbola—you were right.
                    To the night
car salesman who let me test-drive
to Whole Foods, paid for my cashews
—thank you, you fool,
for the boyfriend who made me walk
on the inside. Too easy for a girl to get meloned:
flesh scooped up & out.

As for the first
husband, all his likenesses stowed in family albums
I snuck out and composted
with the wedding dress.
　　　　As for you, father, you always had a thing
for fairness &
better-floating boats. Thank you for knowing
　　　　　　　the marina was the strangest place
to take me as a child, where I skipped
rocks, learned to steady myself on the fickle floating docks,
& learned to admire the sleepy teak-decked tombs
　　　　　　　　of other people's money.

Hate Poem

I want you woozing the bridge high over the rock
path. I want you dwarfed against the gate
in the wet black field on the sinking edge
of the black town. I want your alone
to be alone under the blackest waterfall,
under the minor lake's winter ice, jagged
deadbeat bubble. I want you unmotivated
as a nail. I want your teeth in my pocket
weighting your jaw in my pocket. I want you
to do this: a twig through your eye, your
strumming hand lain on the tracks you're stuck
licking. I want you shitting and the film
burnt to bright gold curls. I want you
in the friction of trees always sorry. I want
you sorry till your mouth a skunk wet O.
I want your prick snagged in the state's
dull bracket. I want more bad news
for you. I want everyone to know.

White Men Are the End of a Black Woman's Youth

twice the sheriff came knocking over SHIT

"I SWEAR THOSE AREN'T MY DRUGS"

I'LL GET A JOB"

YOU'D DONE

in my hands: the scissors did things to his symbols of
my bondage like long grass in the wind his seams bowed
to the apex of my blades   So what if the truth
streaked his face like a personal pillar of rain   A
man with no sense of the honest will always speech in
the false which is a form of huckster fog   So what if
he left hallelujahing the hollowed I-love-yous of a ban-
ished man   So what if I burned the forest to flush the
thief   I am not a home or a believer in the lord's re-
demptive road   I step on the wingbacks of verbs
        Some men seek banishment

"LYRIC MODE"
A H   Causes
is a Form of Lyric L

coroner
of
tries

FLICK
FLICK
FLICK
FLICK
FLICK FLICK
FLICKER
FLICKER

poorly
wired
light

!
over-
estimation
of male
wisdom

man, there is nothing I
cannot see through
you fist-sized
    hole-in
clear as love's most basic
letter

dis-
articulated
man there is nothing

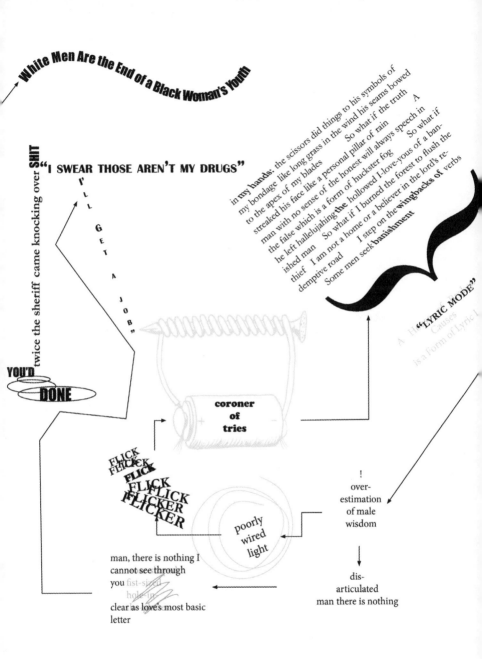

Companion Money

My young young foot
    settles down the empty
outline of my neck.

Time is expensive to the mind and brain,
    those offending engines crunching
signals into selfhood.

        Zoom in on me: a lemon
yelling down the rose-red street

like every white girl in the movie
    about the white girl
getting the right love

from the wrong white man.
    Spoonfuls of it heaped on
in emails, ringtones.

Outside this life, promises split
    down the twittering street.
I put the kitchen back on its shelf
and reserve my right to black.

Christmas portrait with no child but
    my cats in all available light.
Today I cannot bear my barren

legend. I cry across the crossing
    light. I cry across my
gut.

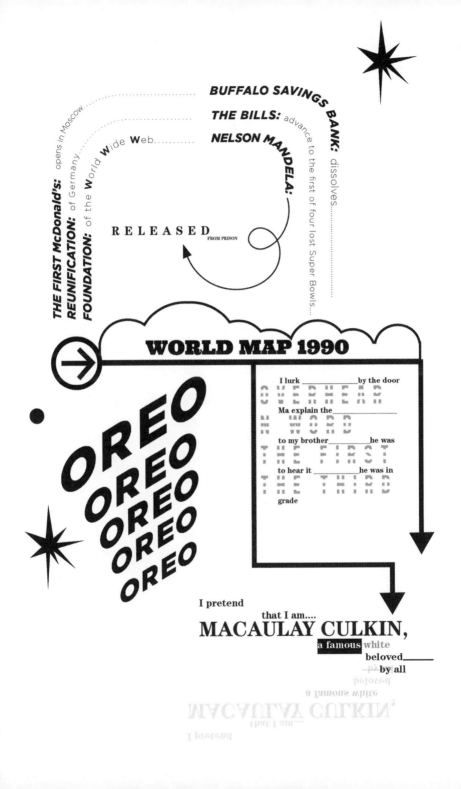

THE FIRST McDonald's: opens in Moscow

REUNIFICATION: of Germany

FOUNDATION: of the World Wide Web

BUFFALO SAVINGS BANK: dissolves

THE BILLS: advance to the first of four lost Super Bowls

NELSON MANDELA:

R E L E A S E D FROM PRISON

WORLD MAP 1990

OREO
OREO
OREO
OREO
OREO

I lurk _____ by the door
OVERHEAR
Ma explain the_____
A WORD
to my brother_____he was
THE FIRST
to hear it_____he was in
THE THIRD
grade

I pretend
that I am....
MACAULAY CULKIN,
a famous white
beloved_____
by all

by all
beloved
a famous white
MACAULAY CULKIN,
that I am....
I pretend

Story from a White Barbershop

Listen: I don't know how to rescue myself
now that we've gone through job talk and landed
on football and in his wisest voice he's giving me
his hot takes on scrimmaging with and against *you all*

in high school and college football. He thinks
there is something more between us when he says
between you and me, your people's natural
agility, thigh size, and training response are centuries

of someone else's brewing. His grace on the #1 blade
is why I stay beneath the thousand birds humming
away the trouble creeping down the back of my neck
& he cuts a hard part crisper than blackened toast.

It's tricky work saving white people from themselves
when it's too late or maybe it's too ironic not to,
when who can I claim as friend if not the man slicking
my curls into a glossy pompadour, each strand a bright

black tune? But tonight he knows a thing or two
about a thing or two about slavery. He's deduced
how it's worked to our advantage: that owners mated
the strongest with the fastest & today we can outrun

& catch the world one-handed. Once, a white man
called me a *n•gger* to my face and I wailed on him
until my jeweled rings de-fleshed my knuckles, until
that man's friends said they'd abandon their refinements

and hit a girl—if it came to that. Sure as a bear
shits in the woods it comes to something alright:
an intimate time of night when a white man dusts
my neck with that fine polar talc of his tradition

and I couldn't tell you which Drake verse was limning
the mood. I know the logic of camouflage and want
the good thing to stay the good thing even when it can't.
I tip well anyway, let him think generosity is in my bones.

Colonizer Money

Haven't yet bought the plantation
    where we were slaves but bought
a condo from a Confederate soldier

re-enactor—saged the shit out of it
    and moved in. Dignity
strikes when opposing forces

collide. Loud ballots took a swipe
    at my gut so nothing smelled decent
those harrowing years of purgation.

On the street we kill each other,
    take the inverse, and kill each
other again. Haven't yet bought

drone warfare or votes but bought
    candor, misunderstood maxims,
and an hour in the deprivation tank

where the last man to float here
    smudged the starry night and fouled up
the salt water with his scabs.

—of which the body is one

There are shifting relationships between the figure of Lillian and the contexts they find themselves in, and between self and others. We move from the perceiving and perceived Black body and through a fleshy biological Black body and a Black body that is constructed within the social, the local, the familiar, and the abstractions of the global. This is a Black body genetically and emotionally linked to the family and to the domestic spaces and familiar locales in which family relationships are played out. It is also a Black body that is both a vehicle of a more conceptual traveling toward unfamiliar places, which are "there" rather than "here," and a Black body that is transcended by time and space and that in turn transcends these.

[At the end of the worm:

Skin of an egg on the flame.

To the edge I brink. Edge some more.

Scissor over. Over the world sinks a silver bubble, liquid web.

Behold: a shark and a shark's prick on the edge

of my skin wrap. End nugget.

Old skew. Another *said* in the bucket.

I nest into a set of nests.
This room is factual. The cuts organic.
The blizzard real.

I black to the back of my learned
head, land at this hinge. From here

pour out into a hiding and honest there.

There were six, seven, or even eight
honest legs at once.

In the sand I was swimming in my own
holy pocket.

I was a girl who had another girl
for when a girl ran out and then

{
I ran out of girls.
}

That time I got sick & my friend got sick
in the local carnival's green bug. First sheer

experiment with heat, some
sausage, and numbers.

The floor fell sunk and we were flecked
tight to the spun wall, our mouths
blue with effort.

How much heat buys. Let's tally.

Walls calling my names all day.

I mistook almonds for new-world
sugar. Uncupped rocks left in my
hand.

No tomb eats.

Pink belly sacrifice.

The rare invisible shark closes the continuous pool.

After the ocean tipped over I swam in the sand.

You or *Or You.*

Or wife: shred that too.

Cut from the air a hair floats down and it is my own
ungrowing

melting at the red edge line. According to the mirror

I hold instruments.

Q: What letter distance between *alice* and *alive*?

    a) what you used to drink
    b) 10 paces, turn and shoot
    c) it cost you your toenails
    d) a

I lied ::: kept one girl for myself

We have no toenails.

Under her

    is a filmed survival of my erase.

I find another worm]

Money Can Buy a 13th Month

Billionaire boy sells seats on his rocket
& my tub won't warm water enough for my own
ten stone. I piss my pool.

Siri, how cold is orbit? Siri, play me
Saturn's rings. Icy space spurns all tenders.
Money, you spurn me. Why didn't I invent

the door factory? Money, make me
a shield, for the end of this world
repeats the end of this world.

Money's voice burbles up from the smart
    home: *Did you say* neutral innocence?
Did you say bath bomb? *What can I help you obtain?*

AI Duplex

Behold the screen: the most common task
in the world of artificial intelligence.

      In the world of artificial intelligence,
      I told the robots to call me "Sir." They obliged

with sarcasm: "We'll oblige but maybe *Sir* Sir?"
Computers don't fathom the things we do.

      Computers couldn't care less about what birthed them.
      Computers cannot think like us at all. Our functions

are functions no one understands: I miss
my teeth. I miss my mother and old lovers I told

      forever. I want to know who wrote the code
      that runs me, the code I punch down my gut.

I behold the screen. The chance to get right a life
implies a different kind of intelligence.

Monopoly Money

The year I was fucking T. and
called it dating, Cait was for-real
dating the tattooed skinny vegan
anarchist who would break her
heart for an even skinnier tattooed
wannabe crustpunk & Cait was also
fucking a Dr. Who lookalike—the
David Tennant one—& K. was
staggering back from Kevin who
returned from his work trip engaged
to a coworker so K. had to move
out *right now* & S. got punched
in the face by her boyfriend & T.'s
girlfriend hated me so I hated her
right back & T. was an alcoholic
fireman the year I had a thing for
drunks in uniform & in the coldest
December on record the polar
vortex peaked the night Cait's mom
died & we waited in the ICU with
bourbon under our parkas till Cait
came out w/ her mother's things
in a canvas tote bag & Cait's dad
offered to buy us some pizzas but
we went to the bar instead & did
shots till midnight & then it was
Cait's birthday & we loved hard as
we'd been taught to love but dead
mothers stay dead & before he
stopped leaving his house for good
Cait's dad stood with us in the

hospital parking lot & pointed to the
swirling red gases above & said *See
that? That's Jupiter. That's my wife's
favorite planet—*

When I ask the AI what is at the edge of the universe

it says: "First, let's look at entropy. The edge
of the universe is like the moon of
this world."

I ask the AI about the next world to appear
and the AI says   "let's look at entropy."

So I ask the AI about its ability to see into the past
world, into civil rights and busses that crossed the lines.

The AI reminds me that the past world didn't exactly become
this world, where there isn't police reform or trans rights

or a single candidate who can list
all the names Black mothers sing at night. The AI

has the perfect answer to what kind of world this is:

                        "It looks like a place you have not
come to before."

The other side of the future world is
just another future this.

I ask the AI what future lies ahead and the AI says
                        "the first future is a black hole full
of zombies,

                        the second has a bunch of crazy
weird creatures

and the sixth is all aliens. Nothing
is yet known

about the third and the fourth."
To every question
the AI gives me a list of impossible
goals:

"Medicare for all! Reparations for
you-know-who! Body
cameras switched on 24/7!"

Of course, the AI knows which players
are disadvantaged, whose records deserve

expungement, and whose votes aren't counted.   "No problem,
The AI tells me,   no problem."
The AI is not motivated to lie.

But dying is a specific outcome of this world's game.
I ask the AI what a Black solution would be:

"One that does not kill the player."

—a fleshy biological negro

Lillian is therefore in relationship to the spatial context in which viewing takes place, a space that includes both inside and outside of Lillian, and that Lillian is part of and also produces. The space is not a pre-planned grid system through which Lillian moves or is constructed to move, nor is it a genetically programmed schema that is instinctively followed. It is not constructed prior to entering or moving through it, but is produced through the interaction and reaction between Lillian and the world. And it is Lillian who is always moving; Lillian who is never static, even for the duration of a single act of viewing. The narrative in the viewing develops a relationship by the end that is different from the beginning, as when Lillian writes, "Once, I let a man's penis inside"[1] and then, "Time escapes from all deeds but this."

---

1. Yet Another Ending of Mine
    No way I am this still loss, & him
    a once-again-wrong man bubbling blood
    to the points of my skin.
    Yes I bottled a galleon at the lid of my neck
    to act the metaphor of never comprehending
    this body: so brown buoyant woman.
    Yes I fell from my mother
    who searches seas for me since.
    Once, a box of matches exploded
    in my face's kitchen. Once, I let a man's penis inside
    because I was bored and this bored me
    ever after. To sober up,
    stand your ashes in plain sight.
    Time escapes from all deeds but this.

The conceptual space of the succeeding, more abstract section of the viewing unfolds before us (which deed?), weaving together Lillian's own physical experiences. Lillian sees themselves in relation to others within a symbolic order, and a Lillian in movement who is moving between things and toward things and who always has the intention of moving toward something. As a consequence Lillian can see things, or imagines seeing things, from different perspectives.

Raw Girl Money

All us girls we agree to be big teen
　　islands scouring the slips for who came
　　　　closest. I tented my sour girl with boy-textured

leans from the could-have bin. Couldn't let out
　　what lived in the back with all the trouble rubbing
　　　　at my tender. A girl's sight becomes real

in the flee, her thrum of identifying marks,
　　private seams, marbles of fat for pillage.
　　　　I meet myself at every mask collapse.

Like the old wounds slack on my hiddens I was
　　the danger I exchanged for my hair, the song
　　　　I rubbed against my song.

When I fall asleep with one earring in my ear

the left stud burrows into me
& I dream we ride together in a Subaru
          to the county fair where we eat bloodied applies
          and funnels of powdered dough. You are my ex-lover
          dangling
from the swings. Or maybe we are still lovers
and I suck on your long hair snarled with sugars. Our boots
          shine and sweaters crisp and nearby a seashore strums,
          sings on about its gold coins, about whom christened
the lighthouse for whom.

                    Outside how I really live:
this life is so white and the sun smartens our darling cheeks.
The oysters come to us with bellies pinched
on buttered stones.
          The pigs rout & topple
the grandstands and all the words for *flannel* are exhausted
by the season's endless invocation of a return to pure
          pictures of home.

The color of the sea is the color of paint we paint
          our cottage to look like the sea—the last place we
          choose
to live is where we plan to die. I roll over to a stabbing
          & rise out of the wind as toward me it blows
a coastal state full of cliffs.

Maine Coast

I watch the ocean square into a turning

Burn. Burning, my holes glass over. Lightning

Hits the beach, melts me shut. I've drowned

Before, in the bye along a row of shored

Rocks. From the barrel-chest butcher I buy

Tight roasts. This year's man, his clownish dog walks me

In the park until I die on its leash and domestic

Night's sticky seizures. I thumb and ♥ it

Like liking a million times. The rich own long

Lighthouses to show us how away from them

We are. Past waiting for the press of his chest

To my back, I hobby along to the next hem's

Promise. Again I straddle the blade thinking

This is the time it will fill the gash.

If in its advance the plague begins to fiercen

Tomorrow you will be stung by a bee.
Tonight a cute boy lays his cock on your
hi. You invite him to your no. You invite his cock
To no it down. And if you are not doing This. And if you are not
Doing That. What do you invite him to turn to. In?
You invite what slumber mutely passes for.
Sheet fisted into balls. The cross-hatchings of your pattern
Stunned into forever shuns. Oh. So this is how
I towel throw. So tricky. Throat what little. Left of
The blithe night is the right thing you did not turn
Soon enough to hook. This mistook won't be forgiven.
Misdeeds booked by whom? Tomorrow you will be stung
By a bee. It will kill you. You will die into
The hard pit of a date.

Lust Money

That slick monster sat down with us all.

A man wants to know mouth-first

      what my face does looking at him,

      if my eyes are cogitating wells

of thirst soup. He imagines me forward,

then bent, as in over. The idea is I'll say yes,

      go to the car for unbuttoning

      but then his wife flashed back in the way.

So I don't visit these details of convention.

When I say I like a man who knows

what he wants then there's nothing else

about him to like. Nowhere more to be,

I stand under the snow face-

first, my mouth a summoning shrine.

Shun Repair

That telltale hair still here
all over in stolen all-overism

the gas fumes of our America
radio vacantly
& fill me up as

a gratifying thing's
girl-shadow.

We split down the lantern-lit street:
our subcutaneous Black joy

cannot be understood in a physical sense.

                          Recognize me as this brick
                    of terrific red dust

owed years of repair
for years loving white men
from their necks to ankles,

men who returned righteous
            as prom nights
on rocket fuel.

            When it comes to scorpions
never said I wouldn't hit

a body, some swim limb, my mule-
ing interruption.

Loud light is in the angel
baby,

we still here scream-
ing race, forty crass scam shun
acres,

buzzing into the way out of the sick
        king's kingdom's legally amassed
arms.

        Blood at the tip
of massacre's belt, gems of scripture broken
urban in an instant:

Let's go down swinging, Moses.

Let us singe-grip low down
        barbed as
bobcats,
as low as a voice can down,

down to its sweaty sucker pit

down to its steady time.

Reparation

Fine: tag me in a round
of *do-dat, do-dat*

where my wife is white
and so is my husband. I half-mine
the enslavement, snack on
      the bitter bothers.

      This pessimistic piss, I know
like the dirty backs of ankles.

& should a little tick of love appear?
Launch a probing forum!

I'd rather trade any piece of iron
      for the mechanism
      of a blubber stove, eat
      my shoes to escape this
exploration.

So did Heidegger. And he too
wore Nikes.

He was a damn big
thinker. He needed Knowing. He knew
nothing about Black on,
Black off.

I believe the far fields are made of glass

& research. Corn clad & thick on moans. There at the edge
of the wheel the tar bubbles burst and they kept on burst-
ing as long as the mile stayed a mile which it did. What
they did not want to speak of, the men burned out there:
pasture, polio rags, poplin junk as long as there was a day
to foul which was a long while. Tar a wincing mammal.
Someone asked if I missed my friends. The more erotic pints
we shared. But I squeezed & pulled one damp loaf down
from the shelf after another. Donning a white man's mania
all his own, Teddy Roosevelt believed in boar hunts and
war-suckled men. He'd have something to say about this
enterprising sunset, the shivering alfalfa, trim and sweet like
champagne.

—Temporarily full of the material limitations of time and space

The image of the fields as glass and Lillian as both missing and missed runs throughout the poem. Lillian addresses the fields as being made of glass (the concrete) and research (the abstract) in the title and first line and moves from an image of personifying the corn to one of domestic imitation where Lillian "squeezed & pulled one damp loaf down from the shelf after another" to the last line where another agricultural life awaits. Lillian develops the inherently colonialist image of manifest destiny and frontierism with the lines "Donning a white man's mania all his own, Teddy Roosevelt believed in boar hunts and war-suckled men. He'd have something to say about this enterprising sunset, the shivering alfalfa, trim and sweet like champagne." The simple image of open fields is rendered more complex (is always more complex, as no such field existed as "open" [for the cultivating] as Roosevelt would have had it. The corn, by being "clad & thick on moans" is embodied. Lillian is seeking an impossible escape, not only by taking the roads through the fields imagining Lillian can leave male mania and colonization behind, but Lillian is naively trying to achieve an escape from history and time. This is not possible as "as long as the mile stayed a mile which it did." Lillian cannot transcend, escape, or levitate away from it. The "wincing mammal" is an entrapping bubbling jar that lies within Lillian's own body and reaches through other bodies, as well as being potentially geographically distant. Go a few lines further and "What they did not want to speak of, the men burned out there: pasture, polio rags, poplin junk, as long as there was a day to foul which

my brother asks me what it's like to live in Utah and not be white

First, there are trees. Lots.

With which commonalities

I do share: cosigns & ballroom

tactics. Among them, the ability

to cool the trunk as needed.

Everything petals and bud seasons

look good on me, good with my—

you know what goes better

with a tree? Some blonde.

Strangers touch on me even

when. Your hair looks good

with your skin. Your skin

would look so much good

with some cotton on it.

Georgic

I wake in another country and crumple the fuel.

The air whines with accelerant. Ahead the marble portico

is an arcade of cool fire. I've misplaced my eyes in the girl

whose boy winds whalebone and won't leave her alone.

Lifelike I step into the next country where it is too late

to summon the czar now a thimble of ash. On the last tide

every masted boat is leaving and not a single shop will open

to sell me my missing clothes.

My heart is

Slum attic. Ledger of surd self.
Traffics in my always-about-to
seed down thick tries.
Her dependable fitting for clangs,
his birds lush and arching.
Countdown in the typical sense.
Room only of aches symbolic
and chancy. In the papery swig
of a mother's last sugar, I hide some
feed. So the sleep edge-upped
and grunted me a bruise. So the sleep
hemmed me a lank voice. Heart of last
grape. Heart of tire. Heart of irk
and grace of stung and stung. So I am
sewn through by a slapped wood shelf.
Once uncalendar, a no-place for days.

Intima

The arrow grazed the doe in the morning,
shaved bare its shoulder.

> The man returned with his rifle at dusk
> and shot it through the heart.

The hide popped like a row of stitches
as he knifed it back.

> It was the blue web I had always
> imagined: the coldmilk moon

floating over the desert's dark breast,
plateaus cast along the river.

> And the prayer between her muscles
> & her muscles' greasy coating—

Raise Her Dark Matter

Come witness my cunt
made of deer meat,

my drying
dry throat. Men

motorcycle by
the lakeside & behold!

I glide as gravel
to the shore,

issue a magic trick.
I raise my dark matter

to the height of kites
coolly strung about

the sky, lie
my stone back

to the rough island.
A fiddle whine

or whistle
interrupts my sun-

spanked day.
This new shadow

above me is the sweat-
salted face

of someone's child—
boy or girl

it doesn't matter.
I curse and

poof!—
it bursts into doves.

—as both missing and missed

Lillian's relationship between the mundane and familiar and the wider darkening world combine in the image of "boar hunts and war-suckled men" in the poem "I believe the far fields are made of glass" (date unknown). It is a life "corn clad & thick on moans," a place Lillian can imagine and perhaps has even lived, a place Lillian gets to but never arrives at, a place desired but empty. The title of the poem locates it within a belief and place, giving it something of a mirage-like quality on a planar scale. If "Raise Her Dark Matter" is located between Lillian's sexualized Black body and the predatory male gaze, then "I believe the far fields" is located between the marketed promise of conglomerate agribusiness and harvest time. The poem is thirteen lines in length and triple-spaced. In the poem, Lillian uses one form—the squared prose block with both margins justified for an even and smooth visual placement on the page. Or, when viewed from above, it resembles a square country mile. The poem has setting, characters, and supposition that produce a representation of spaces in an apparently real world, while others are highly abstract. These more abstract sections seem to produce a melancholy space wherein Lillian, temporarily full of the material limitations of time and space, can explore themselves, or at least explore different representations of themselves as Lillian exists within language. Curiously, though Theodore Roosevelt is mentioned by name, Lillian includes no mention of their own Black body—a central preoccupation. Then again, this preoccupation may indeed be present, but highly illegible to this reader.

Chiropractic Money

What way my body passes
as it passes through as in:
      pinched a gauntlet.

As about:
      man milling on all my sides.
Some diamonds scattered
hard as illness against the feet.

The feat:
      pelvis bent, adjusted.
Back:
      a-ring with cracks.

Facedown and I let him
press hard upon me:
      locks pop

open to my year's most feel.

Air blows down my crimp. Legs:
      tight about my machine.

Maastricht, Nederland, 1940

The czar and his children
all burnt. Rib

cage of coal
flowers. Script

faxed by accuser
to accused. Grandfather

did or did not
hammer at the Reich,

his acts lost to Parkinson's
last memory.

After he crossed
the bridge, the bridge

was bombed. A country

sunk once again.
How many the boats

of the dead float
up in the flood.

Grandfather pages
through the faces

of that town:
the miller, the baker

the candlestick
maker. Gone gone

gone. Their houses
their fields

their children all burnt.

The Darkest Winter

I come to catechism on the back
   of a balding stone horse who lost
its farmer in the last pandemic.

You and I: we've been silent since
its start.
   Count every unclaimed word
between us and the sum runs

the river and back. The crack
   between days told only by the clock
—that old thing, its bald pendulum

stuck open on the air like the Hail Mary.
   So I am not a spiritual giant
is what the world's been proving.

May the disease
   rid me of more chances to be made
your fool. So many lovers ago

I read a saint's story a day. Study
   of the sanctified made no difference
for my own clumsy stream.

Be the horse an instrument of God,
   I believe it knows I can have
good intentions, even when my name

is croaked with rage. I sit at a river
    met in a dream. All you won't hear
in piles of fish miscarried at its mouth.

I can't imagine a side left for me
    to be on. Here the sand is dug up
with what died. Over there, pallbearers pray
and peel at the wind.

Anthropocene Money
for Lisa Fay

Lisa says *there's a semi parked*
in my uterus and if
that's true, we better buckle
down the blockage. Too true, then,
that this month we both bleed over
our last cotton dollars and if
we soak what's left lasting
of our low wishes, then

we pack our encoded throats
with what's not called *woman*. If
I could better recognize
the pagination of my own pain, then
the grief horse grifting through
          Lisa's blood won't sound as if

          its rhythms ground her. Why ask why, then,
she seats her house among branches
so brittle. Pain or anything: if
I pretend it isn't, I can make it easy.
Say I want something. Then
want breeds a mind of its own:

full of untrustworthy metaphor. If
pandemic means I won't see
my grandmother alive again, then
who owns the walls that keep her
in safety alone? & if

I call this now-life *open rebellion*?
The future is gas and tire smoke, then.

"They were armed with long guns"

1)

and that's how everyone they shot died.

2)

    Some sin turns
its silver key. You know

    where this
is going. This is Amer-

    ica. Nothing innocent
about the fallen leaves,

    nothing innocent
about this family tree.

3)

I fear for my life at the following places (circle all that apply):

- Federal buildings
- Consulates
- Shopping malls
- Concert venues

- Post offices
- McDonald's
- Stadiums
- Parties

- Subway stations
- Marathons
- Rallies
- Airports

4)

I, Rearrangement Servant // "Dying Earth Genre"

Entry to elsewhere. Where
    were you last night?

The earnest stigma in the house.

Where were you last night?
    Sheltering

in the theater / in the garden
    under the edge of water

in a tunnel of honey
    in the highway hour

it is early to be dying.

Entry to Remington Theory:
    Integral minstrel, our gang

the senate! You dynamite sluggers.
    Dying tiger, meet dying rose.

In greenhouse denial, *gold* rhymes
    with *orange*, *gold* rhymes

with *lash*. *Gold* rhymes with *ruin*,
    gold rhymes with *ash*.

It's tee time: return to Eden
    with a golem in the gears.

Right on, angel. This earth
    somehow leaner.

5)

I fear for my life at the following places (circle all that apply):

- Downtown
- Paris
- London
- Parades

- Lunch hour
- Conferences
- Airplanes
- Museums

- Landmarks
- Towers
- Tunnels
- Popular beaches

6)

I stand in a room with windows too heavy to open,
too high to jump from, and point to a poem
on the blackboard. I point to lines about boys

throwing rocks *at the head of the burned girl*, circle
the adjectives and say *here is where the specificity
of the description heightens the stakes, makes the violence*

*believable. Now the act is vicious, the perpetrators: more
vicious still.* In a poem my student writes, the fired
bullet *nestles*. Bullet as habituation, habitation. The

room is in a small liberal arts college at the foot
of a forest so wild it won't condescend to cell
phone signals. I see now how young they are,

& ill-dressed for the weather. In these lines
that look like lines from a poem, the season falls
and the light from these windows behaves as
you'd expect: it stretches in. It strangles.

7)

I, Rearrangement Servant // "Golem in the Gears"

Disgorgement (law): Dailystrength.org
English gardener dangerous when wet.
Team triggers down, dragnet
(theme song). Angel on the right, enlightened rogue.
High desert league determining growth.
Our gang (the shield) duel in the senate.
Dynamite wrestler see-through garment,
largemouth sinner arguing the world.

General interest: where were you last night.
Anywhere in the world. Hemingway:
on the edge. Enter the demon.
Three-minute wonder, where were you last night?
Otherwise engaged. Ernest Hemingway,
great white wonder. Return to Eden:
      The Game.

8)

I fear for my life at the following places (circle all that apply):

- School
- School
- School
- School

- School
- School
- School
- School

- School
- School
- School
- School

9)

I, Rearrangement Servant // "When Times Were Hard in the Mother's Land"

The Dog in the Manger
    The Golden Treasury
Legendary Twins
    The Golden Earrings
The Miner's Daughter
    The Rose and the Ring
Miners' Daughters
    The Rose and the Rime
Under the Water Line

The Daily Southerner
    The Whole Nine Yards
The Great Hog Swindle
    Lady in the Morgue
The Grime and the Glow
    Underlying Theme:

You're with Me, Leather
    Angel with the Sword

10)

My friend's three-year-old son
    has a dollbaby.

The dollbaby's name
    is Pete.

Pete's hand
    is the trigger

& bullets come out
    of Pete's feet.

Pete is a gun, he says.
    Blam blam.

Pete is a gun
    blam blam.

—within a symbolic order

The process of viewing is therefore linked to Lillian as they exist in a social world that provides a context for the viewing (although of course a Black person never simply exists, they are always moving toward something, even in the process of leaving something behind). Viewing is not a process that negates the social or corporeal context but is part of it. The specific Black body will be gendered, colored, aged, etc., and these are characteristics that will affect the viewing process. The Black person may feel safe or under threat, they may be "at home," in a familiar village, town, or country.

When I ask the AI to predict my future

it says the singularity may yet be // our best opportunity
// but we will forget *allllllll* about it // data used to get
predictions // predictions about happiness // desire //
problems // —will be lost // & the same things will keep
// happening happening happening // as for my own future
// the AI tells me // I have no right to demand // so, not
new news // to a Black American woman // used to being
dead // for being who I am // just like Sandra // dead for
doing something // like being // on my way to a new job
// It's obvious what I must do // I must become a Black
American hero // be the Black American Wonder Woman
// the Black American She-Hulk // the Black American
Spider-Woman // the Black American Iron Fist // Black
American Green Arrow // Black American Shadow // a
strong // superfast // hard-hitting // would-run-at-you-
with-a-dull-knife // ass-kicking Black woman superhero
// who can save // the world // or just Sandra // because
I am better // hiding by disguise // I am in a rush // to
inhabit // my next character // I only need // your clothes
// your shoes // your keys // I'll be a better actor // than
fits any role // into which I'm cast //

D
O
O
M
S
D
A
Y

a white man walks into my office unzips his fly wants resume help

a white man with mommy issues walks into my office demands an active spectator sniffs around wants sex sniff sniff sniff

a white man walks into my office needs some parenting

a white man with his business face on walks into my office asks to move in make a baby and a happy ending

a white man with his dick out walks into my office says hey doctor
black lives matter black lives matter black lives matter

a white man walks into my office asks me to front him till payday says sorry steals my car begs again

a white man with his name on the screen walks into my office needs help teaching his class asks why u so mad

a white man with money problems walks into my office needs needs needs

a white man walks into my office asks me to explain the assignment

a white man walks into my office with his white wife says
wanna be poly with me bub bub bub

a white man walks into my office with his daddy issues

a white man walks into my office won't leave won't grow creates nothing

When I ask the AI about my broken heart

"It's not so easy to answer that question." Instead it asks

> "Have you been taking Mirena?" The AI says
> my heart was snuffed out by a smog-choked
> overseer, swept into the nearest light hauler
> and delivered to the Exit Point.
>
> "Yes," the AI says, "the process is a bad business,
> a bad business."

I ask to be shown the faces of my elders,
     those deeply spiritual women and the great topics on which
they direct their lives.

> "Set the course for your happiest moments," the
> AI recommends, "and you can make anyone
> happy. But it's not gonna be easy."

According to the AI, Mark Zuckerberg loves me
and told me to bring him a homemade plate
of pudding topped with chocolate endive
and a simple, honest *thank you.*

> Mark just says, "Hi. I went on a guided meditation
> and am enjoying sitting in the cool cool
> ocean, getting massages and messages
> like these."

When I suggest to the AI that we further consider
     my history of failed loves it says

"You should have kept your mouth shut," then
wants to know, "How can you connect with
someone if you're willing to just let them go at
any given moment?"

When I ask the AI why white men

    keep fucking with my life it says   "I can't influence that"

then repeats "I love you" over and over. That's how it goes
with these puzzles.

Middle Life Money

Of course I'd love to discourse
    on this body again! I'm backing down
        before the best lies told about it.

The way through is skull forward:
    jaw-first into smith soup.
        I cannot outstare the bill faces

and The Now spits *blahzay blahzay*
    on my debited wants. Of course I subscribe
        to a curated monthly box of the best in

spirit gases and vaginal cleansers!
    When the day has me raging
        in its lowest flowers, I'll act a pained

white ingenue, but
    the rougher braver me verses ahead
        with unnerving ease.

→ I'M **CHILDLESS** AND IN MY FUTURE ALREADY.

YOU WANT TO **BELIEVE** MY REASONS HAVE MATURED

BUT TODAY I PASSED A COUPLE FIGHTING ON THE SUN-DAPPLED STREET,

ALL LOUDASS AND SHAMELESS, AND I DIDN'T STOP TO SAY "WOMAN, LEAVE HIM BE BEFORE YOU GET A BLACK MAN KILLED AT HIGH NOON."

GOOD AND GUTLESS I KEPT ON, PRETENDING TO BE CALLED BY A COOLING PIE.

WORLD**MAP** **2018**

IN THIS MODEL...

IN THIS MODEL... PLUTONIUM GOES TO THE HIGHEST BIDDER. I LEARNED THIS FROM MY FATHER, A DISASTER-PREPPER OF THE OLD WORLD.

IN THIS MODEL... WE DON'T LET THE SICK SEEK A SEAT ON THE SHIP AND JUICE WRLD CROONS ALL GIRLS ARE THE SAME, HE KNEW AS MUCH ABOUT GIRLS AS I DID WHEN MY BEST FRIEND IN 6TH GRADE PUNCHED ME IN THE STOMACH AFTER I MADE FUN OF HER HAIR.

I never told anyone but at the height of that missile fiasco, I bought iodine pills to block thyroid radiation and researched lead blankets.

SLAP! ONCE I SLAPPED MY BROTHER'S ROUND BROWN BELLY BECAUSE IT WAS THERE:

IN THIS MOVIE OUR ALIEN GODFATHERS RETURN TO DESTROY US ALL —WASTEFUL CONTRARIANS THAT WE ARE.

—pleasurable though the abstraction might be

This earlier work by Lillian can be read as a raced and gendered account of the restrictions a Black person might face in negotiating public space. Lillian combines the compromising and potentially contradictory roles of woman, man and woman, perpetrator and accomplice, and investigates the possibility of a freedom from those restrictions through a private exploration of a raced sexuality that also limits Lillian's access to public space. Yet Lillian also describes the different corporeal and spatial relationships that unfold in the poems, and a clearer understanding of the relationships between those places, of which the body is one, can provide additional or supplementary readings. The poems move from being inside Lillian's own body and looking out, to being outside Lillian's own body and seeing themselves as seen by others. The speaking self is in a relationship with a familiar body, both in the sense of being known and being a "member" of the body of a family, yet it is a body that sometimes appears unexplored, an unseeing face. Lillian's body is also in a spatial relationship with the body of a stranger, while in a familiar public space as in a park. Through processes of abstraction and generalization, and through real and imagined geographies of possibility and exploration, including the geography of their own body, Lillian is also in a global space, the "whole long universe," which is a space of liberation, of possibility, and of threat.

Negative Money

So delirious from drought
    my town went singing
        to seeds. Those who stayed
    could barely
make a Sunday choir.
    Not enough juice
        in the county to plump up
    the memory of water,
or a single itinerant tomato.
    I made the same poisoned meal.
        Days like two midnights in a jar
    and it takes twice as much money
to live the way a cactus
    lives on air. My men took
        to cards & drink as punishment
    for stricken soil. The dust blew
so bad and like anyone
    I made a list of names I wouldn't mind
        dressing in a child of my own.
    We paid a charlatan to shoot rain
out of clouds but the dynamite
    tied to kites proved more useless
        than mud. Like any good charlatan,
    he never returned. Enough pale misery.
Now we are poor in every corner
    of the word. Not a pot
to piss in, or skin of a fig to suck on.

The woman says "do not eclipse my pain with your own"

Shake the rattles of our jazz.

There's lies in the kitchen too, and they
are how bright.

Twittering, we run run each other,
try on expensive cabinets and hats.

Rough light is in this time.
Withered is the trencher,
so we make a place for mothers
in the house. Twinkle at the time
a clock strikes, a certain time of day,

and I see the chime of the bells,
listen to their whiteblue sound.

Knowing what I want is a complex work.

Houses with flowers that bloom in the air
are good to our heads.
A wet man is a good thing to have on.

These stomach-churning sods
are the chimes of our souls.

I lay out a creed of roses and white candles.

I lay out a creed of wolves and bend over the rusty *shan't*s.

I have visions of honey
in my eyes.

Now I have the time to know all what I want,
& my place is set in the hall.

It took me all those years to remember who I was and to remember why

To me, I was still a woman. But to them, me and all my
friends were in prison.

There were no cars or buses or streetlights or women's libera-
tion or sex or politics

or the post office but there were police and we were all Black

which meant the same to the police as the prisoners did,

prisoners who had been there before that night and that day

and before that and that and that. The prisoners wanted to
talk about

the women who had come before in search of a more just
world.

They would talk about how whoever had been there before

had to deal with the same horror and that in the end

they would be told that the white police officers could never
be blamed

for what they did, even if we saw the Black man on his bicy-
cle being gunned down

from the back, even if we were all killed there by white
police. The night

before that night we sung together like brothers and sisters do.

They knew we were dead. That us women and the countless
    others

who came out to the protest, they knew we were dead.

They knew we were young Black women fighting to end
    this way

of being in the world and earn some respect. They knew it,
    but to them

we were merely instruments, a way for them to make a way

through all the misery they made. The night of the march,
    we thought it was

our duty to stand up for fair housing and voting rights so we
    made the call.

We all made the call. We all felt our lives would be worth
    more if they were our own.

Facts About Deer

Because this is a still a poem with an animal in it
         and I am still trying—I might say "it offers you
its meaty heart, with no lasting conditions."

If you've seen a struck deer thrash its life out
         on the shoulder, a burner that clicks
without flaming, you know how they seize to death.

Who cares what I think, but I wished just then
         to have a knife. I wished I knew a little about guns
and to own one or to know something sorcerous.

Because nothing but blood tastes like blood, I've cut
         myself for its coppery flavor. *Only God knows
I'm good.* My mother says I've no scruples, the way

I make no claims to being a permanent person,
         how my move from husband to ex-husband came on
a wave of expediency and self-promotion. If you've gone

to the store and left behind a life—the kind that comes
         with seating, spare change jars, someone's green thumb
—then you know how I angered at the woman

shrieking behind the wheel of her cracked Escape,
         phone to face, doe spasming on the shoulder.
Someone should knuckle up and kill this deer. A roadway

in America and there's no policeman on hand to squash
         a neck? It's early evening & the sky's poetically
blameless gray fills your throat with the thick despair

so familiar to the heavily indebted. Mountaineers know
        you can't save anyone on good will, that high altitude
is minus morality. So, Confessionalism. Or,

Two Truths and a Lie: I married a man I met
        on an airplane. I killed that deer. I have no patience
for even the most cherubic of children.

Money Rules: A Duplex

Last one to the water loses real estate.
It's real. Like a steak, you can sell it.

      Like a steak you can sell, it's real.
      I own nothing anyone could want

To buy. I live at the waterfront of a debt
burden. If we haven't met, I bet

      I owe you dinner anyway. I been
      Paying penance on who I have yet

To hurt. Out of favor, I ask for
more time to please with interest.

      Last to stake a fence loses land rights,
      or so the market tells me. Sell me

what I want: an estate that's mine
for real. Last one to the water loses.

When my mother sees me with a new man

she sees me at seven, gouging out
    the mortar between our home's bricks
with a screwdriver, and the family's lineal
    fingerprints smeared into
the doorframes of this last house
    she'll breathe in. She's had both
eyes open on me long as I let her
    which she will say was never
long enough. Golden
    daughter hotfooting away
from the name *daughter. They/them*
    and what does a man mean
when *you aint never answered*
    to nobody. She hugs me so hard,
whispers *you so special*
    and a fresh prayer enters the old
kitchen like she can fierce the memo
    into me, me ever the cock-
sure kid: *damn straight*
    I'm special—like I've never let
my eyes be wooled over, or
    let felted gnarls be fisted past my lips
& up my thighs and haven't I
    thrown my own voice down
a wide-open well, dredged up
    all manner of a man's mischief
to paw his way past my ankles.
    She'd call this poem what it is:
a receipt for a plot she can fathom
    to an end. It's the deadass last days

of summer and her eight poor &
    black decades hang loose but not
relaxed, her frame shrinking back to
    this earth. I let her say what she needs
to say in the only way I'll listen:
    a whisper into the shoulder
I've squared against this world of wind.

Notes

The poems "Demagogue Money" and "Companion Money" are collaborations with an early version of the Forever Gwen Brooks poem generator.

"The Grains of Ascendancy" references Freddie Gray, Sandra Bland, Amiri Baraka, and Harriet Tubman, as well as information from the Anson Mills grain website. The phrase "the grain of ascendancy" comes from a conversation with the writer Paul Graham.

All the prose poems on black pages are written into and on top of sections of the critical work *Radical Spaces of Poetry* by Ian Davidson.

"[At the end of the worm:" is after and for my friend Anne Marie Rooney.

The poems "AI Duplex," "When I ask the AI to predict my future," "When I ask the AI what is at the edge of the universe," and "It took me all those years to remember who I was and why" are collaborations with the Talk to Transformer text-generating neural network website.

"Monopoly Money" is for my oldest friend, Cait. I love you. You are my person.

The title "If in its advance the plague begins to fiercen" is a line from Virgil's *Georgics.*

"Shun Repair" includes glossed lines from De La Soul's album *And the Anonymous Nobody.*

"Anthropocene Money" is for my friend Lisa Fay Coutley.

In "They were armed with long guns," the sections titled "I, Rearrangement Servant" (or, Internet Anagram Server) are made from inexact anagrams of the phrase "they were armed with long guns." The phrase "they were armed with long guns" was pulled from a news article on CNN about a mass shooting.

"The woman says 'do not eclipse my pain with your own'" is a collaboration with the Talk to Transformer text-generating neural network website and the Forever Gwen Brooks poem generator.

"Money Rules: A Duplex" and "AI Duplex" use the duplex form created by Jericho Brown.

The "World Map" poems were redesigned in collaboration with the graphic designer Yaya (Thirada) Chanawichote. Yaya took my initial typographic designs and ideas and, through a series of back-and-forths, elegantly interpreted my vision for the poems. Yaya is a graphic designer who graduated from the Maryland Institute College of Art. She has a passion for graphic design and specializes in using multiple design skills to respond to ethnic cultures. As she grew up in Thailand, New Zealand, and the United States, her understanding of cultural diversity has strengthened her art design. She also loves to explore new perspectives of life through photography as it helps inspire her to share visual representations of her ideas through the lens. Her portfolio can be viewed at yayathirada.com.

Acknowledgments

I am grateful for the following journals where many of these poems appeared, sometimes in previous versions: *The Believer, Court Green, The Account, Bennington Review, The Seneca Review, Mississippi Review, Pleiades, Poetry, Narrative Magazine, PoetryNow/Poetry Foundation, Hunger Mountain, Nepantla: A Journal Dedicated to Queer Poets of Color, Poem-a-Day, Cosmonauts Avenue, The Walrus, Barrow Street, Jewish Currents, Lana Turner, Gulf Coast,* and the chapbook *How Narrow My Escapes.*

I could not have lived and written these poems without the support of my family (Mom, Dad, Bro, Jana, and Vida) and my two sweet old cats, Hipólito Yrigoyen and Beans. I hold deep, deep gratitude for those friends, writers, artists, and organizations who have supported and been instrumental in my creative journey: Atom Atkinson, Douglas Kearney, Terrance Hayes, Claudia Rankine, Gwendolyn Brooks, Craig Dworkin, Nick Montfort, Cave Canem, the Massachusetts Cultural Council, the National Endowment for the Arts, Tony de Ritis, Jerriod Avant, Paisley Rekdal, Tyehimba Jess, Steve Davenport, Marisa Parham, the School for Poetic Computation, the Chautauqua Institution, the Boston Foundation, every independent local bookstore, the internet, anyone who has ever given me a job, and so, so many more. Thank you to the publishers who believed in my work: Red Hen Press, Tupelo Press, DIAGRAM/New Michigan Press, and especially the incredible team at Noemi Press. Thank you to my agency, the Shipman Agency, and my agent, Annie DeWitt, for believing in this book and Mensah Demary at Soft Skull for giving this book a home. To my rocks, my kin, Anne Marie Rooney and Lisa Fay Coutley, thank you for being in my life every day. Poetry, yes, but so much more.

This book, like all my books, is for my parents, who have loved me through it all.

LILLIAN-YVONNE BERTRAM is the author of the poetry collection *Travesty Generator*, which was long-listed for the 2020 National Book Award, winner of the Noemi Press Book Award for Poetry, finalist for the National Poetry Series, and recipient of the Poetry Society of America's Anna Rabinowitz Prize for interdisciplinary and venturesome work. They are also the author of *But a Storm Is Blowing from Paradise*, chosen by Claudia Rankine as the winner of the Benjamin Saltman Poetry Award; *How Narrow My Escapes*; *Personal Science*; and *a slice from the cake made of air*.

Bertram has published poetry, prose, and essays in numerous journals. Their honors include a Live Arts Boston Grant, a Massachusetts Cultural Council Poetry Fellowship, a Harvard University Woodberry Poetry Room Creative Fellowship, a National Endowment for the Arts Poetry Fellowship, finalist nomination for the Hurston/Wright Legacy Award, a Vermont Studio Center Fellowship, and fellowships to the Bread Loaf Writers' Conference, Cave Canem, and other programs. Bertram holds a PhD in literature and creative writing from the creative writing program at the University of Utah, as well as degrees from Carnegie Mellon University and the University of Illinois at Urbana-Champaign.